I Like Tickles

a book about bodily autonomy and respect

Sarah Steinberg

STRIKEFORCE DESIGN
PORTLAND, OREGON

www.strikeforcedesign.net

No part of this publication may be reproduced in whole or in part, or stored in a retrieval system, or transmitted in any form or by any means, electronic, mechanical, photocopying, recording, or otherwise, without written permission of the publisher.   All rights reserved.

ISBN-13: 978-1725558878

Copyright © 2018 by Sarah Steinberg

I Like Tickles

was written to help explain to my two-year-old son that it is important to respect our tolerant, but frustrated, dog. I hope it will inspire more toddlers and preschoolers to both request and provide physical respect.

I like **tickles**.
Tickles make me laugh!
When I'm done, I say, "No more,"
and mama stops **tickling**.
I get to decide when I'm done being **tickled**.

Papa doesn't like **tickles**.

He asks for a **high five** instead.

I listen.

Not everyone thinks tickles are fun.

Puppy doesn't like **tickles**.

She shows her teeth to say "**No touching**."

I keep my hands off of puppy.

Puppy is in charge of who touches her.

I like kisses! Kisses make me smile.
But if puppy kisses too much, I say "STOP",
and puppy listens.
I can say I'm all done, even if I liked it.

Mama likes kisses! Kisses make her feel loved.
Sometimes we all want to kiss mama at the same time.
We make sure she's happy and smiling
when we give kisses.

My uncles like **hugs**.
Sometimes I'm not in the mood to do any more **hugging**, even though I love them.
I **wave** goodbye instead.

My friend and I like to hug.

When we're done, we let go.

We both decide when to hug

and when to be finished.

Kitty doesn't like **hugs**.

She hisses to say "don't touch me."

I let her **walk away**, even if I want to pet her.

Kitty gets to say she doesn't want to be hugged.

I like **snuggles**!

When I'm done, I like to get up and run around.

Mama doesn't mind.

I'm in charge of when I want to **snuggle**.

Mama likes **snuggles** too -
but when she's cooking, she needs space to work.
If she says "I'm busy," I listen.
Mama likes **snuggling** best when she is relaxed.

Puppy likes **pets** from Papa.
If I try to **pet** her, she growls,
or finds another place to rest.

I can pet Papa instead. He won't go away!

Everyone likes different kinds of touching.

Sometimes we say "Yes please!"
and sometimes we say "No thanks."

Some days we're in the mood to hug,
and some days we just say goodbye.

Sometimes we're in the mood to pet,
and sometimes in the mood to be petted.

We listen to each other.

We are all in charge of our bodies.

Many thanks

(hugs or otherwise) to my first enthusiastic readers - the moms of a certain secret society that need not be named - for your encouragement, edits, and love, and to my mom, who suggested I stop yelling, start writing, let her referee the dependants while I scribbled the first draft in sharpie and crayons at the kitchen table.

About the Author

Sarah Steinberg is a watercolor artist and writer raised in New Jersey. She's spent many years designing and illustrating buildings, and is now shifting focus to her first preoccupation, writing and illustrating. Sarah has been telling stories as long as she can remember, to a tape recorder, her siblings, and many computers. She lives in Portland, Oregon, with her husband, son, and underemployed border collie.

Visit her at www.strikeforcedesign.net.

Made in the USA
San Bernardino, CA
20 May 2019